Traveler Said

*291 inspiring
quotations from the*
San Francisco Chronicle's
Quotable Traveler
column

Larry Habegger

WOODEN WALKWAYS PRESS
San Francisco

Cover design, interior design, and page layout:
Bonnie Smetts

Cover photographs: camels and the Giza pyramids,
Egypt; Tibetan prayer flags on a mountain pass in
Sikkim, India: Larry Habegger

Library of Congress Cataloging-in-Publication Data
available upon request.

ISBN: 978-1-60952-024-3
E-ISBN: 978-1-60952-025-0

First Edition
10 9 8 7 6 5 4 3 2 1
Printed in the United States of America

INTRODUCTION

FOR FIVE AND A HALF YEARS as each season changed, I settled in for a visit with my favorite travelers. From books, essays, letters, articles, proverbs, and other sources, I ferreted out quotes that inspired me and that I trusted would inspire my readers in the *San Francisco Chronicle*'s Travel section. The newspaper ran my column, "The Quotable Traveler," from 2010 to 2016, each week featuring the words of wisdom of a traveler I had found in my research. It was a pleasure and an honor to provide this column.

I got in the habit of sending in my choices in batches of thirteen, so it became a seasonal experience for me. On the cusp of a new season, I'd muse along with the world's great travelers, spanning centuries and the globe, and savor the brief time I got to spend with them. Invariably they entertained me, kindled my wanderlust, reminded me how vibrant the world is and why seeking out experiences near and far remains an uplifting and important pursuit.

I hope the quotations that follow will engage you, move you, and ignite the urge to head out into the world again and again. At the very least, they should allow you to pause a moment and gaze at the horizon, knowing that limitless possibilities await you there.

Larry Habegger
San Francisco, California

SUMMER

"A good traveler has no fixed plans, and is not intent on arriving."

—*Lao Tzu (600 BC-531 BC), Chinese Taoist Philosopher, founder of Taoism; Poem 27, "Tao Te Ching" (The Way of Life)*

"The only way of catching a train I ever discovered is to miss the train before."

—*G.K. Chesterton (1874-1936), English writer, known for the "Father Brown" mysteries; "Tremendous Trifles" (1909)*

"Travel is fatal to prejudice, bigotry, and narrow-mindedness, and many of our people need it sorely on these accounts. Broad, wholesome, charitable views of men and things can not be acquired by vegetating in one little corner of the earth all one's lifetime."

—*Mark Twain, "The Innocents Abroad" (1869)*

"I have wandered all my life, and I have also traveled; the difference between the two being this, that we wander for distraction, but we travel for fulfillment."

—*Hilaire Belloc (1870-1953), Anglo-French writer and historian, author of "The Path to Rome" (1902)*

"The foliage on the Midsummer poles had wilted. The leaves had turned a pale green and curled like chips of old paint. The flower wreaths hung in dull, tired bands from the cross-arms. It would be autumn soon, and we should have already reached the Arctic Circle, seen the midnight sun, and begun the long ride south across Finland before the cold weather returned. But it didn't matter. The sun was out, and the sky was clear."

—*Allen Noren, author of "Storm: A Motorcycle Journey of Love, Endurance, and Transformation" (2000)*

"It isn't the road ahead that wears you out—
it is the grain of sand in your shoe."

—*Arabian proverb*

"I stand under a Connemara sky slashed
with rain and ask the old farmer the nettled
question, while leaning against the old
drystone wall, 'Where does this road go?'
He leans against the old wall of clabbered
stones, and whistles for his sheepdog to
follow him home, then replies, 'To the end,
lad. To the end.'"

—*Phil Cousineau, writer, filmmaker, teacher,
tour leader, and author of numerous books
including "The Art of Pilgrimage" (1999) and
"The Book of Roads" (2015, 2000)*

"What's yer road, man—holyboy road,
madman road, rainbow road, guppy road,
any road? It's an anywhere road for anybody
anyhow."

—*Jack Kerouac, author of several books
including "On the Road" (written in 1951,
published in 1957)*

"Come to the edge," he said.
They said, "We are afraid."
"Come to the edge," he said.
They came.
He pushed them…
And they flew.

> —*Guillaume Apollinaire (1880-1918), French poet, playwright and art critic, credited with coining the word "surrealism"*

"Travel not only stirs the blood—it also gives birth to the spirit."

> —*Alexandra David-Neel (1868-1969), French explorer and writer, author of more than 30 books including "My Journey to Lhasa" (1927) and "Magic and Mystery in Tibet" (1929)*

"Applying for a difficult visa turns any traveler into a coward."

> —*Thurston Clarke, American author of 11 books, including "Equator" (1988) and "Searching for Crusoe" (2001)*

"To awaken alone in a strange town is one of the pleasantest sensations in the world."

—*Freya Stark (1898-1998), British explorer and author of more than two dozen books, including "The Valleys of the Assassins" (1934) and "A Peak in Darien" (1976)*

"We travel, some of us forever, to seek other states, other lives, other souls."

—*Anaïs Nin (1903-1977), French author famous for her published journals, "Diary, Vol. 7, 98"*

"I love travel with a passion, the good days and the bad. And I don't care to analyze the reasons too deeply—running to, running from, inner journeys, outer journeys, fear of commitments, fear of dying, fear of missing out on things—all of the above, or none. Who cares?"

—*David Yeadon, English author and illustrator of more than 20 books, including "The Way of the Wanderer" (2001) and "At the Edge of Ireland" (2009)*

AUTUMN

"I had imagined a border scene similar to Nouadhibou.... As we approached the crossing—a compound of featureless cement buildings ringed by barbed wire—the Iranian sitting beside me watched me slip a crisp $100 bill between the pages of my passport. 'Put that away,' he warned, 'or they will throw you in prison without a second thought.'"

—*Jeff Greenwald, author of several books, and a performance artist, from "The Size of the World" (1995)*

"Glastonbury in summer, one of its residents told me, is 'like living in a house of tarot cards.'"

—*Catherine Watson, former travel editor of the Minneapolis Star-Tribune, from the story "Where the Veil Thins" in "Home on the Road" (2007)*

"Soldiers, from the summit of yonder pyramids 40 centuries look down upon you."

—*Napoleon Bonaparte, speech to his troops in Egypt, July 21, 1798*

"There are people everywhere who form a Fourth World, or a diaspora of their own.... They share with each other, across all the nations, common values of humor and understanding.... They are easily grateful. They are never mean.... They are exiles in their own communities, because they are always in a minority, but they form a mighty nation, if they only knew it."

—*Jan Morris, Welsh author of more than 40 books, from "Trieste and the Meaning of Nowhere" (2001)*

"Great joy in camp. We are in view of the ocean, this great Pacific Ocean which we have been so long anxious to see."

—*Capt. Meriwether Lewis, diary entry from the Lewis and Clark Expedition, November 7, 1805*

"We left Kabul on 10 July ('Probably for ever,' we said, jesting in the tedious fashion that explorers employ to keep up their spirits)."

—*Eric Newby, a dean of British postwar travel writing, from "A Short Walk in the Hindu Kush" (1957)*

"Thus I left the Philippines. But the Philippines did not so easily leave me. For months, I could not get the country out of my head: it haunted me like some pretty, plaintive melody."

—*Pico Iyer, essayist and author of many books, from "Video Night in Kathmandu" (1988)*

"There is no end to the process of getting your life back—eventually you have to come down from the mountain. And as any good mountain climber knows, the real success is surviving the descent."

—*Alison Wright, photojournalist and author, from "Learning to Breathe: One Woman's Journey of Spirit and Survival" (2008)*

"What is traveling? Changing your place? By no means! Traveling is changing your opinions and your prejudices."

—*Anatole France (1844-1924), French novelist and winner of the Nobel Prize in Literature, 1921*

"Don't think there are no crocodiles because the water is calm."

—*Malay proverb*

"We know from the first step that travel is often a matter of confronting our fear of the unfamiliar and the unsettling—of the rooster's head in the soup, of the raggedy edge of unfocused dread, of that cliff face that draws us willy-nilly to its lip and forces us to peer into the void."

—*Tim Cahill, essayist and author of many books, from the essay "Exotic Places Made Me Do It," in "Outside" (March 2002)*

"There is something about safari life that makes you forget all your sorrows and feel as if you had drunk half a bottle of champagne."

—*Karen Blixen, a.k.a. Isak Dinesen (1885-1962), Danish novelist and author of "Out of Africa" (1937)*

"I just love it. I could spend my life arriving each evening in a new city."

—*Bill Bryson, author of many books, from "Neither Here Nor There: Travels in Europe" (1992)*

WINTER

"My ideal vacation consists of sitting in a chair beneath an umbrella on my patio, reading books of adventures I would never consider attempting unless I was escaping from something."

—*Isabel Allende, author of many novels and nonfiction works, from "My Invented Country: A Nostalgic Journey through Chile" (2003)*

"I dislike feeling at home when I am abroad."

—*George Bernard Shaw (1856-1950), Irish author and playwright, winner of the Nobel Prize in Literature (1925) and an Oscar (1938) for his adaptation for the screen of his play "Pygmalion"*

"His surgical knowledge was excellent; he knew the location of the vital organs quite accurately from frequent cutting up of bodies for eating."

—*Frederick O'Brien (1869-1932), American author, from "White Shadows in the South Seas" (1919)*

"People don't talk about death in Parma. They wait for it. They visit cemeteries on a weekly and sometimes daily basis. But talking about death is bad taste and bad luck."

—*Wallis Wilde-Menozzi, American poet and author of "Mother Tongue: An American Life in Italy" (1997)*

"You are unlikely to have a startling adventure if you never take a more hazardous journey than a train ride from your house to the office."

—*W. Somerset Maugham (1874-1965), English author of numerous plays, short stories, travel books and novels, including "The Moon and Sixpence"*

"I had gotten to Lower Egypt, and was heading south, in my usual traveling mood: hoping for the picturesque, expecting misery, braced for the appalling."

—*Paul Theroux, American author of many books, from "Dark Star Safari" (2003)*

"A man who has not been in Italy is always conscious of an inferiority, from his not having seen what it is expected a man should see."

—*Samuel Johnson (1709-1784), British poet, essayist, moralist, literary critic, biographer, editor and lexicographer*

"What does it mean to internalize the sound of church bells, fireworks at six in the morning? Burros' braying, Mexican curses and words of praise? The days and weeks gain rhythm, unfold in time."

—*Tony Cohan, American lyricist and author, from "On Mexican Time" (2000)*

"Tenzing and I had spent a good part of the previous night quaffing copious quantities of hot lemon drink and, as a consequence, we arrived on top with full bladders. Having just paid our respects to the highest mountain in the world, I then had no choice but to urinate on it."

—*Sir Edmund Hillary (1919-2008) on scaling Mt. Everest in 1953, from "View from the Summit" (1999)*

"At day's end we'd draw the Land Rover behind a dune for shelter and prepare some slim waterless meal—tomatoes and tinned sardines and bread as dry as dust. Muggleton sheltered in the vehicle or under it, and I lay on the roof while the persistent wind slowly covered us in sand as fine as the air."

—*Ann Jones, American author, from "Looking for Lovedu: Days and Nights in Africa" (2001)*

"'When in Rome' is all right up to a point, and that point is generally accepted to be well passed when it comes to, say, headhunting with the natives of Papua New Guinea."

—*Jeremy Seal, British author and broadcaster, from "A Fez of the Heart: Travels around Turkey in Search of a Hat" (1995)*

"If I am asked 'what is the use of climbing this highest mountain?' I reply: No use at all—no more than kicking a football about, or dancing, or playing the piano, or writing a poem, or painting a picture."

—*Francis Younghusband (1863-1942), British army officer, explorer and chairman of the Mount Everest Committee who encouraged George Mallory to attempt the first ascent of Everest*

"Take those two words, gold and pleasure, for a lantern, and explore the great cage of Paris."

—*Honoré de Balzac (1799-1850), French novelist and playwright best known for "The Human Comedy," his multi-volume collection of interlinked novels about French society*

"The Columbia depressed me with its barren grandeur. Never had I seen such a large body of water in such an arid space. I had always associated water with life, but here, sun-burnt hills on either side were relieved only by rock and sage."

—*Thomas Swick, American editor and author, from "A Way to See the World" (2003)*

SPRING

"Most travel, and certainly the rewarding kind, involves depending on the kindness of strangers, putting yourself into the hands of people you don't know and trusting them with your life."

—*Paul Theroux, American author of many books, from "Ghost Train to the Eastern Star" (2008)*

"Like all great travelers, I have seen more than I remember, and remember more than I have seen."

—*Benjamin Disraeli (1804-1881), British prime minister and novelist, from "Vivian Grey" (1827)*

"To cross the Strait of Gibraltar towards Morocco is to leave behind many things. Jittery nerves, for instance. And quirky Western notions about the way things out to be."

—*Laurie Gough, Canadian author, from "Kite Strings of the Southern Cross" (1999)*

"You can never go home again, but the truth is you can never leave home, so it's all right."

—*Maya Angelou, American poet and author, from an interview with Jackie Kay, 1987*

"Except for certain situations involving science, warfare or divine prophecy, there is never really any practical reason to go wandering off into the desert—and this is likely the very reason why so many people are inclined to do it."

—*Rolf Potts, American author, from "Marco Polo Didn't Go There" (2008)*

"Half the fun of the travel is the esthetic of lostness."

—*Ray Bradbury, American author of numerous essays, stories and books, including "Fahrenheit 451"*

"The Paykan swerved to the side of the road and a portly gentleman levered himself out from the driver's seat and steamed across the pavement towards me, like the *Titanic* on a pressing engagement with an iceberg. I was in Iran and I was about to be kidnapped. "I am a guide. I speak English…."

—*Tony Wheeler, English author and cofounder of Lonely Planet Publications, from "Badlands: A Tourist on the Axis of Evil" (2007)*

"And that's the wonderful thing about family travel: it provides you with experiences that will remain locked forever in the scar tissue of your mind."

—*Dave Barry, American humorist, from "Dave Barry's Only Travel Guide You'll Ever Need" (1991)*

"There is nothing like a hit of solitude to help you sort out what's in your head and figure out what's important in life. Again I stayed behind and let everyone go ahead in order to walk alone."

—*Michel Moushabeck, musician, author and publisher of Interlink Books, from "Kilimanjaro: A Photographic Journey to the Roof of the World" (2009)*

"Though we travel the world over to find the beautiful, we must carry it with us or we find it not."

—*Ralph Waldo Emerson (1803-1882), American philosopher, essayist and poet*

"Certainly, travel is more than the seeing of sights; it is a change that goes on, deep and permanent, in the ideas of living."

—*Miriam Beard (1901-1983), American author and essayist*

"People travel to faraway places to watch, in fascination, the kind of people they ignore at home."

—*Dagobert D. Runes (1902-1982), philosopher and author, from "Treasury of Thought: Observations over Half a Century" (1967)*

"Travel, in the younger sort, is a part of education; in the elder, a part of experience."

—*Francis Bacon (1561-1626), English philosopher, statesman, scientist, jurist and father of the scientific method*

SUMMER

"If you reject the food, ignore the customs, fear the religion and avoid the people, you might better stay home."

—*James Michener (1907-1997), American author of more than 40 books, including "Tales of the South Pacific," which became the basis for the musical, "South Pacific"*

"Though they carry nothing forth with them, yet in all their journey they lack nothing. For wheresoever they come, they be at home."

—*Sir Thomas More (1478-1535), English lawyer, consultant to Henry VIII, a Catholic saint, from "Utopia" (1516)*

"Soar, eat ether, see what has never been seen; depart, be lost, but climb."

—*Edna St. Vincent Millay (1892-1950, American poet, playwright, and winner of the Pulitzer Prize for Poetry in 1923, from "On Thought in Harness"*

"Don't listen to what they say. Go see."

—*Chinese proverb*

"The soul of the journey is liberty, perfect liberty, to think, feel, do just as one pleases."

—*William Hazlitt (1778-1830), English literary critic and philosopher, from "Table Talk" (1822)*

"Travel makes one modest. You see what a tiny place you occupy in the world."

—*Gustave Flaubert (1821-1880), French novelist, author of many books including "Memoirs of a Madman" and "Madame Bovary"*

"Keep moving."

—*Hunter S. Thompson (1937-2005), American "gonzo journalist" best known for his book "Fear and Loathing in Las Vegas"*

"There are no foreign lands. It is the traveler only who is foreign."

—*Robert Louis Stevenson (1850-1894), Scottish novelist best known for the books "Treasure Island," "Kidnapped" and "Strange Case of Dr. Jekyll and Mr. Hyde"*

"Travel like Gandhi, with simple clothes, open eyes and an uncluttered mind."

—*Rick Steves, American writer, publisher, filmmaker, Europe expert best known for his Rick Steves' line of guidebooks*

"All journeys have secret destinations of which the traveler is unaware."

—*Martin Buber (1878-1965), Austrian-born Jewish philosopher best known for his philosophy of dialogue*

"To travel is to live."

—*Hans Christian Andersen (1805-1875), Danish author most famous for his children's stories such as "The Ugly Ducking," "The Little Mermaid" and "The Snow Queen"*

"Did you ever notice that the first piece of luggage on the carousel never belongs to anyone?"

—*Erma Bombeck (1927-1996), American humorist most famous for her syndicated newspaper column that ran from 1965 to 1996 and regular appearances on "Good Morning America"*

AUTUMN

"It is not down in any map; true places never are."

—*Herman Melville (1819-1891), American novelist and essayist, from "Moby-Dick" (1851)*

"One's destination is never a place, but rather a new way of looking at things."

—*Henry Miller (1891-1980), author of numerous books including "Tropic of Cancer" (1934), from "Big Sur and the Oranges of Hieronymus Bosch" (1957)*

"Traveling is like flirting with life. It's like saying, 'I would stay and love you, but I have to go; this is my station.'"

—*Lisa St. Aubin de Teran, English novelist, winner of the Somerset Maugham Award for "Keepers of the House" (1982)*

"Own only what you can carry with you; know language, know countries, know people. Let your memory be your travel bag."

—*Alexander Solzhenitsyn (1918-2008), Russian novelist and dissident, author of many books including "The Gulag Archipelago" (1973)*

"Go forth on your path, as it exists only through your walking."

—*Saint Augustine (354-430), philosopher and theologian revered by both Catholics and Protestants, who lived in the Roman Africa Province, modern day Algeria*

"When you travel, remember that a foreign country is not designed to make you comfortable. It is designed to make its own people comfortable."

—*Clifton Fadiman, (1904-1999), American author, editor and host on radio and TV of the popular quiz show "Information Please!"*

"The open road is a beckoning, a strangeness, a place where a man can lose himself."

—*William Least Heat-Moon, American writer, from "Blue Highways" (1982)*

"Going from — toward; it is the history of every one of us. It is a great art to saunter."

— *Henry David Thoreau (1817-1862), American author of many books including "Walden," from "Journal," April 26, 1841*

"A ship in a harbor is safe, but that's not what ships are built for."

— *William Shedd (1820-1894), American Calvinist theologian and editor of the collected works of Samuel Taylor Coleridge (1894)*

"Look at the stars lighting up the sky: no one of them stays in the same place."

— *Seneca (4 BC-65 AD), Roman stoic philosopher, statesman, dramatist, and tutor and advisor to Emperor Nero*

"Only by going alone in silence, without baggage, can one truly get into the heart of the wilderness. All other travel is mere dust and hotels and baggage and chatter."

— *John Muir (1838-1914), American naturalist, in a letter to his wife, July 1888*

"Discretion rebelled against the folly of my plans, but as usual met a crushing defeat at the hands of curiosity."

—*Richard Halliburton (1900-1939), American writer and adventurer, from "The Royal Road to Romance" (1925)*

WINTER

"The earth belongs to anyone who stops for a moment, gazes and goes on his way."

—*Colette (1873-1954), French novelist and performer, and author of "Gigi" (1944)*

"To travel is to discover that everyone is wrong about other countries."

—*Aldous Huxley (1894-1963), English essayist and author of "Brave New World" (1932)*

"If a man be gracious and courteous to strangers, it shows he is a citizen of the world."

—*Francis Bacon (1561-1626), English philosopher, statesman, scientist, lawyer and pioneer of the scientific method*

"Don't tell me how educated you are, tell me how much you have traveled."

—*The Prophet Mohammed*

"But, at such an age, you will never return from so long a journey. What care I for that? I neither undertake it to return, nor to finish it: my business is only to keep myself in motion, whilst motion pleases me.

—*Michel de Montaigne (1533-1592), French statesman, essayist and father of Modern Skepticism, from "Of Vanity"*

"Hotel cooking in the island is so appalling that a stretcher may profitably be ordered at the same time as dinner."

—*Patrick Leigh Fermor (1915-2011), English scholar, author and travel writer writing about Trinidad in "The Traveller's Tree" (1950)*

"I think I would rather cross the African continent again than write another book. It is far easier to travel than to write about it."

—*David Livingstone (1813-1873), Scottish medical missionary and subject of the famous quote, "Dr. Livingstone, I presume?" From the Introduction to "Missionary Travels in South Africa" (1857)*

"The tourist is part of the landscape of our civilization, as the pilgrim was in the Middle Ages."

—*V.S. Pritchett (1900-1997), British critic, essayist, professor, biographer and short story writer, from "The Spanish Temper" (1954)*

"To travel in ignorance of a region's history leaves you unable to understand the 'why' of anything or anyone."

—*Dervla Murphy, Irish author of more than 20 travel books over the past 40 years, including "Full Tilt" (1965) and "The Island That Dared" (2008)*

"In traveling; a man must carry knowledge with him, if he would bring home knowledge."

—*Samuel Johnson (1709-1784), British poet, essayist, moralist, literary critic, biographer, editor and lexicographer*

"One can only really travel if one lets oneself go and takes what every place brings without trying to turn it into a healthy private pattern of one's own."

—*Freya Stark (1893-1993), British adventurer and author of more than two dozen travel books, from "Riding to the Tigris"*

"If people and their manner of living were alike everywhere, there would not be much point in moving from one place to another."

—*Paul Bowles, (1910-1999), American expatriate composer, translator and author of many books, including the novel "The Sheltering Sky," from "Their Heads Are Green and Their Hands Are Blue" (1963)*

SPRING

"It is a cliché to say that life is a journey, but it is true. What shore did you wash up on when you were born? What well-worn coat of many colors will you be wearing at your end?"

—*James O'Reilly, publisher of Travelers' Tales books, from "The Best Travel Writing 2011"*

"You go away for a long time and return a different person — you never come all the way back."

—*Paul Theroux, American author of many books, from "Dark Star Safari" (2003)*

"If there is any inherent value to travel at all, it is that while wandering one reinforces his empathy with the earth."

—*Georgia Hesse, travel writer and founding travel editor of the former "San Francisco Sunday Examiner & Chronicle"*

"I haven't been everywhere, but it's on my list."

—*Susan Sontag (1933-2004), American essayist and novelist, author of many works including "The Way We Live Now"*

"The person susceptible to 'wanderlust' is not so much addicted to movement as committed to transformation."

—*Pico Iyer, essayist and author of many books, including "The Man Within My Head" (2012)*

"I came to realize that I traveled best when I traveled no faster than a dog could trot."

—*Gardner McKay (1932-2001), American TV/film actor, sculptor and author, from "Journey without a Map" (2009)*

"No one realizes how beautiful it is to travel until he comes home and rests his head on his old, familiar pillow."

—*Lin Yutang (1895-1976), Chinese author,*

*inventor and translator of classic Chinese
works, from "A Trip to Anhwei"*

"Travel has taught me that different people find different truths to be 'self-evident' and 'God-given.' It humbles me. It stokes my curiosity. It helps me celebrate rather than fear the diversity on our planet."

—*Rick Steves, filmmaker, tour guide and author
of the best-selling "Rick Steves' Travel Guides"*

"When you're traveling, you are what you are right there and then. People don't have your past to hold against you. No yesterdays on the road."

—*William Least Heat-Moon, American writer,
from "Blue Highways" (1982)*

"Travel and change of place impart new vigor to the mind."

—*Seneca (4 BC-65 AD), Roman stoic
philosopher, statesman, dramatist, and tutor
and advisor to Emperor Nero*

"A journey is best measured in friends, not in miles."

—*Tim Cahill, American essayist and author*

of many books, including "Lost in My Own Backyard" (2004)

"There is a change that takes place in a man or a woman in transit. You see this at its most exaggerated on a ship when whole personalities change."

—*John Steinbeck (1902-1968), American novelist and Noble Prize winner, from "Steinbeck: A Life in Letters" (1975)*

"Our battered suitcases were piled on the sidewalk again; we had longer ways to go. But no matter, the road is life."

—*Jack Kerouac (1922-1969), from "On the Road" (1957)*

SUMMER

"Indeed there exists something like a contagion of travel, and the disease is essentially incurable."

—*Ryszard Kapuscinski (1932-2007), Polish journalist and author, from "Travels with Herodotus" (2004)*

"We are all tourists now, and there is no escape."

—*Paul Fussell (1924-2012), American historian, professor, and author, from "Abroad: British Literary Traveling Between the Wars" (1980)*

"The Pacific Crest Trail wasn't a world to me then. It was an idea, vague and outlandish, full of promise and mystery. Something bloomed inside me as I traced its jagged line with my finger on a map. I would walk that line..."

—*Cheryl Strayed, from "Wild: From Lost to Found on the Pacific Crest Trail" (2012)*

"Trains do not depart: they set out, and move at a pace to enhance the landscape, and aggrandize the land they traverse."

—*William Gaddis (1922-1998), American novelist, from "The Recognitions" (1957)*

"Traveling is a brutality. It forces you to trust strangers and to lose sight of all that familiar comfort of home and friends."

—*Cesare Pavese (1908-1950), Italian poet and novelist, author of many books including "The Prison" (1949)*

"The first condition of understanding a foreign country is to smell it."

—*Rudyard Kipling (1865-1936), British poet, Nobel laureate, and author of many books including "Kim" (1901)*

"A wise traveler never despises his own country."

—*Carlo Goldoni (1707-1793), Venetian playwright and librettist, author of "Servant of Two Masters"*

"The use of traveling is to regulate imagination by reality, and instead of thinking how things may be, to see them as they are."

—*Samuel Johnson (1709-1784), British poet, essayist, moralist, literary critic, biographer, editor and lexicographer, from "Letter to Hester Thrale," 21 September 1773*

"May your trails be crooked, winding, lonesome, dangerous, leading to the most amazing view. May your mountains rise into and above the clouds. May your rivers flow without end..."

—*Edward Abbey (1927-1989), American author, essayist and environmentalist, from "Desert Solitaire" (1968)*

"Make voyages! Attempt them! There's nothing else."

—*Tennessee Williams (1911-1983), American playwright, from "Casino Real" (1953)*

"Traveler's heart
Never settled long in one place
Like a portable fire."

—*Basho (1644-1694), Japanese poet and haiku
master*

"The first experience can never be repeated.
The first love, the first sunrise, the first
South Sea island, are memories apart and
touched a virginity of sense."

—*Robert Louis Stevenson (1850-1894), Scottish
novelist best known for the books "Treasure
Island," "Kidnapped" and "Strange Case of
Dr. Jekyll and Mr. Hyde," from "In the South
Seas" (1896, published posthumously)*

"Every perfect traveler always creates the
country where he travels."

—*Nikos Kazantzakis (1883-1957), Greek writer
and philosopher, best known for his 1952
novel "Zorba the Greek"*

AUTUMN

"This was the moment I longed for every day. Settling at a heavy inn-table, thawing and tingling, with wine, bread, and cheese handy and my papers, books and diary all laid out; writing up the day's doing, hunting for words in the dictionary, drawing, struggling with verses, or merely subsiding in a vacuous and contented trance while the snow thawed off my boots."

—*Patrick Leigh Fermor (1915-2011), British scholar, soldier and author of many books, including "A Time of Gifts" (1977)*

"People don't take trips—trips take people."

—*John Steinbeck (1902-1968), American Nobel laureate, author of many books, including "The Grapes of Wrath" (1939)*

"On a long journey, even a straw weighs heavy."

—*Spanish Proverb*

"In San Francisco it has long been dark. It is nearly 10 at night there. Here, endless sun. I have done everything. Sleep. Prayers. And I finished Hesse's 'Siddhartha.' Nothing changes the endless sunlight. And in this light the stewardesses come with questionnaires that we must all fill in. Why do we travel?, etc."

—*Thomas Merton (1915-1968), American mystic and writer, flying to Asia in 1968*

"There are still ceremonial fights in rural Bolivia in which people are killed, and many young Bolivians are surely glad to be free of their parents' superstitions; but to the foreigner passing through, this often translates as a kind of sunlit antiquity."

—*Pico Iyer, American author of many books, from "Sun After Dark" (2004)*

"Sheesh. I can't believe you are complaining. We're in Timbuktu man. TIMBUKTU!"

—*Teresa O'Kane, upbraiding her husband, Scott, in "Safari Jema" (2011)*

"A visitor quickly learns that to ensure he receives accurate, relevant information, never ask a question which can be answered with a 'yes' or 'no.' 'Yes' can mean 'Yes, I heard you' without a modicum of understanding of its content."

—*Steve Van Beek, American expat author and filmmaker, from "Thailand Notes" in "Travelers' Tales Thailand" (2002)*

"What saves a man is to take a step. Then another step."

—*Henri Guillaumet (1902-1940), French aviator, quoted by fellow pilot and author Antoine de Saint-Exupery (1900-1944) in "Wind, Sand and Stars" (1939)*

"Whenever the thought of annihilation enters the mind, it's far better to kiss the dog and the rest of the family good-bye and set out for parts unknown."

—*Mary Bartnikowski, American photographer and writer, from "Everyday Naked" (1998)*

"When good Americans die they go to Paris."

—*Oscar Wilde (1854-1900), Irish writer and poet, from "A Woman of No Importance" (1893)*

"He who will travel far spares his steed."

—*Jean Racine (1639-1699), French dramatist, from "Les Plaideurs (The Litigants)," I. 1.*

"I remember Pang La, Tibet as a stark, stony place where I spent an eternity shaking like a leaf in an inadequate sleeping bag, kept awake by helpless crescendos of clattering teeth and the gulping of air by my oxygen-starved tent mate. The only relief was getting up and urinating under an astonishing sky, at once the darkest and brightest I'd ever seen."

—*James O'Reilly, American editor and writer, from "Notes from the Roof" in "Travelers' Tales Tibet" (2003)*

WINTER

"Travel is like a good, challenging book: it demands presentness—the ability to live completely in the moment, absorbed in the words or vision of reality before you."

—*Robert D. Kaplan, American journalist and author, from "Being There," an essay in the Nov. 2012 issue of "The Atlantic"*

"It's easier to find a travel companion than to get rid of one."

—*Art Buchwald (1925-2007), American humorist, longtime columnist for The Washington Post*

"The moment you commit to a journey it takes on a unique life of its own, which no amount of agonizing in advance can foresee."

—*Jason Elliot, British author, from "An Unexpected Light: Travels in Afghanistan" (1999)*

"The car is considered a life-support system—a survival capsule for outer space—but if it breaks or gets bogged down, life suddenly enjoys less support than it might with more primitive transportation."

—*David Darlington, American author, from "The Mojave" (1996)*

"Love thrives especially well in exotic locales."

—*Diane Ackerman, American author, from "A Natural History of Love" (1994)*

"Though the names are still magic—Amazon, Nile, Congo, Mississippi, Niger, Platte, Volga, Tiber, Seine, Ganges, Mekong, Rhine, Rhone, Colorado, Euphrates, Marne, Orinoco, Rio Grande—the rivers themselves have almost disappeared from consciousness in the modern world."

—*Robert Hass, former U.S. poet laureate, from his Introduction to "The Gift of Rivers" (2000)*

"Trains are the stuff of stories inside and out. From windows I have seen lovers embrace, workers pause from their travail. Women gaze longingly at the passing train; men stare with thwarted dreams in their eyes."

—*Mary Morris, American author, from "Wall to Wall" (1992)*

"I cannot tell you what immense impression Paris made on me. It is the most extraordinary place in the world."

—*Charles Dickens (1812-1870), English author and social critic, in a letter to Count D'Orsay (1844)*

"Travel offers the opportunity to find out who else one is, in that collapse of identity into geography I want to trace."

—*Rebecca Solnit, American author, from "A Book of Migrations" (1997; 2nd edition 2011)*

"Here's what I love about travel: Strangers get a chance to amaze you."

—*Tanya Shaffer, American author, playwright and actor, from "Somebody's Heart Is Burning" (2003)*

'Tis a good rule in every journey to provide some piece of liberal study to rescue the hours which bad weather, bad company, and taverns steal from the best economist."

—*Ralph Waldo Emerson (1803-1882), American essayist, lecturer and poet, from "English Traits" (1856)*

"To live in Europe as an American, even if you speak the language and can read a wine list, is to be an immigrant and thus an outsider. Most expatriates go through each day with a touch of homesickness, as if it were a low-grade infection."

—*Matthew Stevenson, American writer and banker living in Switzerland, from "Letters of Transit " (2001)*

"It is safer to wander without a guide in an unmapped country than to trust completely a map traced by men who came only as tourists and often with biased judgment."

—*Marie-Louise Sjoestedt (1900-1940), French linguist and literary scholar, from "Gods and Heroes of the Celts" (English translation published posthumously in 1949)*

"The midsummer light seduced us into staying up late. Some nights we never slept at all. We sat on our Blazo stools in our big canvas tent, brewing up cup after cup of coffee and hot Tang, and, as Callimachus put it, 'tired the sun with talking as we sent him down the sky.'"

—*David Roberts, American wrier and climber, writing about Alaska's Brooks Range in "Escape Routes" (1997)*

SPRING

"I nurture and honor my inner nomad by surrounding myself with reminders of my journeys."

—*Lavinia Spalding, American author and editor, from "Writing Away" (2009)*

"The trips that change our lives are the ones where nothing specific happens, and one can remember, 27 years later, every day."

—*Pico Iyer, American author of many books, from the essay "The Trip that Changed My Life" on Gadling.com*

"Even disasters—there are always disasters when you travel—can be turned into adventures."

—*Marilyn French (1929-2009), American feminist and author of "The Women's Room" (1977)*

"The longing provoked by the brochure was an example of how a lengthy and ruinously expensive journey might be set into motion by nothing more than the sight of a photograph of a palm tree gently inclining in a tropical breeze."

—*Alain de Botton, British author of many books, from "The Art of Travel" (2004)*

"I have been on the road all my life. My father was convinced that travel was good for the mind, while my mother believed it good for the soul."

—*Phil Cousineau, American author and filmmaker, from "The Art of Pilgrimage" (2000, 2012)*

"There is wisdom in turning as often as possible from the familiar to the unfamiliar: it keeps the mind nimble, it kills prejudice, and it fosters humor."

—*George Santayana (1863-1952), Spanish-American philosopher, poet, essayist and novelist, from the essay "The Philosophy of Travel" (1964)*

"I didn't need to see the gamelan orchestra to hear its music, and I didn't need to be in Bali to have Bali in me. It was already there, gonging and trilling and booming, rice paddy blooming, and it always would be."

—*Don George, American writer and editor, on leaving Bali, from the essay "Unexpected Offerings on a Return to Bali" on Gadling.com*

"There are places that feel like the answer to why we travel in the first place, why we bother to trespass, sometimes crossing lines that look like fences. This Cairo souk is one of my few."

—*Colleen Kinder, American journalist, from the story "Blot Out" in "The Best Women's Travel Writing, Volume 9" (2013)*

"For in their hearts doth Nature stir them so, Then people long on pilgrimage to go, And palmers to be seeking foreign strands, To distant shrines renowned in sundry lands."

—*Geoffrey Chaucer, medieval English poet, from "The Canterbury Tales"*

"Social critics who proclaim that 'real travel' is dead are just too lazy to look for complexities within an interconnected planet."

—*Rolf Potts, American journalist and author, from "Marco Polo Didn't Go There" (2008)*

"The whole object of travel is not to set foot on foreign land; it is at last to set foot on one's own country as a foreign land."

—*G. K. Chesterton (1874-1936), English literary and social critic, author, poet, and playwright, in the essay "The Riddle of the Ivy" from "Tremendous Trifles" (1920)*

"I soon realized that no journey carries one far unless, as it extends into the world around us, it goes an equal distance into the world within."

—*Lillian Smith (1897-1966), American novelist and civil rights activist, best known for her novel "Strange Fruit" (1944)*

"A visit to India is always met with warnings of 'touts,' but the India I have often experienced is one where more people want to help than harangue."

—*Meera Subramanian, American writer, from her story "Mucking About" in "The Best Women's Travel Writing, Volume 9" (2013)*

SUMMER

"I did not tell half of what I saw, for I knew I would not be believed."

—*Marco Polo, on his deathbed in 1324*

"A train isn't a vehicle. A train is part of the country. It's a place."

—*Paul Theroux, American author of many books, from "Riding the Iron Rooster" (1988)*

"Traveling is one way of lengthening life."

—*Benjamin Franklin, from a letter from Paris, Sept. 14, 1767*

"Travel does what good novelists also do to the life of everyday, placing it like a picture in a frame or a gem in its setting."

—*Freya Stark (1893-1993), British adventurer and author of more than two dozen travel books, from "Riding to the Tigris" (1959)*

"We all have our time machines. Those that take us back are memories. And those that carry us forward, are dreams."

—*H.G. Wells (1866-1946), English author of many books, including "The Time Machine"*

"Perhaps, then, this was what traveling was, an exploration of the deserts of my mind rather than those surrounding me."

—*Claude Lévi-Strauss (1908-2009), French anthropologist and author of many books, from "Tristes Topiques" (1955)*

"It is good to have an end to journey towards; but it is the journey that matters, in the end."

—*Ursula K. Le Guin, American novelist and poet, from "The Left Hand of Darkness" (1969)*

"An adventure is simply physical and emotional discomfort recollected in tranquility."

—*Tim Cahill, American essayist and author of many books, including "Lost in My Own Backyard" (2004)*

"Each time I go to a place I have not seen before, I hope it will be as different as possible from the places I already know."

—*Paul Bowles (1910-1999), from "Their Heads Are Green and Their Hands Are Blue" (1963)*

"The gladdest moment in human life, methinks, is a departure into unknown lands."

—*Sir Richard Burton (1821-1890), English explorer, diplomat, essayist and author of many books, including "First Footsteps in East Africa (1856)*

"I could spend my life arriving each evening in a new city."

—*Bill Bryson, American author of many books, from "Neither Here Nor There: Travels in Europe" (1992)*

"Travel is like living in a new world, so free, so fresh, so vital, so careless, so unfettered, so full of interest that one grudges being asleep."

—*Isabella Bird (1831-1904), English explorer, naturalist and author of many books, from a letter to her sister, 1871*

"Travel, which was once either a necessity or an adventure, has become very largely a commodity, and from all sides we are persuaded into thinking that it is a social requirement, too."

—*Jan Morris, Welsh historian, essayist and author of many books, including The Pax Britannica Trilogy (1968-1978)*

AUTUMN

"If travel is like love, it is, in the end, mostly because it's a heightened state of awareness in which we are mindful, receptive, undimmed by familiarity and ready to be transformed."

> —*Pico Iyer, American author of many books, from the essay "Why We Travel" on Salon. com (2000)*

"It requires less courage to be an explorer than to be a chartered accountant."

> —*Peter Fleming (1907-1971), British author of several books and older brother of Ian Fleming of James Bond fame, from "Brazilian Adventure" (1933).*

"Travel seems to me a splendid lesson in disillusion—chiefly that."

> —*D.H. Lawrence (1885-1930), English novelist, poet, playwright, essayist and literary critic, in a letter to Mary Cannan from Tahiti, Aug. 31, 1922*

"There is nothing like returning to a place that remains unchanged to find the ways in which you yourself have altered."

—*Nelson Mandela, from "A Long Walk to Freedom" (1994)*

"To see ten thousand animals untamed and not branded with the symbols of human commerce is like scaling an unconquered mountain for the first time, or like finding a forest without roads or footpaths, or the blemish of an axe."

—*Beryl Markham (1902-1986), English-born Kenyan aviator and author, from "West with the Night" (1942)*

"There are only two emotions in a plane: boredom and terror."

—*Orson Welles (1915-1985), American actor, director, writer and producer*

"Not all those who wander are lost."

—*J.R.R. Tolkien (1892-1973), English author of classic fantasy novels including "The Hobbit," from "The Lord of the Rings" (1949)*

"A man sees in the world what he carries in his heart."

—*Johann Wolfgang von Goethe (1749-1832), German author, poet and politician*

"A journey is a person in itself; no two are alike."

—*John Steinbeck (1902-1968), American Nobel Prize winner and author of many books, including "The Grapes of Wrath" (1939)*

"I pack my trunk, embrace my friends, embark on the sea, and at last wake up in Naples, and there beside me is the stern fact, the sad self, unrelenting, identical that I fled from."

—*Ralph Waldo Emerson (1803-1882), American philosopher, essayist and poet*

"Travel can be one of the most rewarding forms of introspection."

—*Lawrence Durrell (1912-1990), expatriate British novelist, poet and travel writer best known for his tetralogy of novels, "The Alexandria Quartet" (1957-1960)*

"Perhaps travel cannot prevent bigotry, but by demonstrating that all peoples cry, laugh, eat, worry, and die, it can introduce the idea that if we try and understand each other, we may even become friends."

—*Maya Angelou, American poet and author, from "Wouldn't Take Nothing for My Journey Now" (1993)*

"Peculiar travel suggestions are dancing lessons from God."

—*Kurt Vonnegut, Jr. (1922-2007), American author of many books, from "Cat's Cradle" (1963)*

WINTER

"A traveler has no power, no influence, no known identity. That is why a traveler needs optimism and heart, because without confidence travel is misery."

—*Paul Theroux, American author of many books, from "The Tao of Travel" (2011)*

"Trust in Allah, but tie your camel."

—*Arab proverb*

"Twenty years from now you will be more disappointed by the things you didn't do than by the ones you did do. So throw off the bowlines, sail away from the safe harbor. Catch the trade winds in your sails. Explore. Dream. Discover."

—*Mark Twain*

"A traveler without observation is a bird without wings."

—*Moslih Eddin Saadi (1210-1292), a major Persian poet of the medieval period*

"We lean forward to the next crazy venture beneath the skies."

> —*Jack Kerouac (1922-1969), author of several books, from "On the Road" (written in 1951, published in 1957)*

"I was born lost and take no pleasure in being found."

> —*John Steinbeck (1902-1968), American Nobel Prize winner and author of many books, including "The Grapes of Wrath" (1939), from "Travels with Charley" (1962)*

"The sight of the huge world put mad ideas into me, as if I could wander away, wander forever, see strange and beautiful things, one after the other."

> —*C.S. Lewis (1898-1963), Irish-born British novelist and academic best known for "The Chronicles of Narnia" (1949-1954), from "Till We Have Faces" (1956)*

"They should tell you when you're born have a suitcase heart, be ready to travel."

—*Gabrielle Zevin, American screenwriter ("Conversations with Other Women," 2007) and author ("Elsewhere," 2005)*

"The end is nothing, the road is all."

—*Willa Cather (1873-1947), American novelist best known for her Pulitzer Prize-winning novel "One of Ours" (1922) and "My Antonia" (1918), from "Obscure Destinies" (1932)*

"Climb the mountains and get their good tidings. Nature's peace will flow into you as sunshine flows into trees."

—*John Muir, (1838-1914), American naturalist, from "Our National Parks (1901)*

"Do not wait for life. Do not long for it. Be aware, always and at every moment, that the miracle is in the here and now."

—*Marcel Proust (1871-1922), French novelist, critic and essayist best known for his novel "Remembrance of Things Past" (1913-1927)*

"For my part, I travel not to go anywhere, but to go. I travel for travel's sake. The great affair is to move."

—*Robert Louis Stevenson (1850-1894), Scottish novelist best known for the books "Treasure Island," "Kidnapped" and "Strange Case of Dr. Jekyll and Mr. Hyde," from "Travels with a Donkey in the Cevennes" (1879)*

"What I find is that you can do almost anything or go almost anywhere, if you're not in a hurry."

—*Paul Theroux, American author of many books, from "The Happy Isles of Oceania" (1992)*

SPRING

"Do not follow where the path may lead. Go instead where there is no path and leave a trail."

—*Ralph Waldo Emerson (1803-1882),*
American philosopher, essayist and poet

"An adventure is only an inconvenience rightly considered. An inconvenience is only an adventure wrongly considered."

—*G. K. Chesterton (1874-1936), English literary*
and social critic, author, poet, and playwright,
from "All Things Considered" (1908)

"The darkest thing about Africa has always been our ignorance of it."

—*George Kimble, early 20th century American*
geographer

"The search for novelty, for what is alien, for what stretches our imagination and awes our mind—this is what the traveler travels for."

—*Peter Whitfield, English author, historian and poet, from "Travel, A Literary History" (2011)*

"Lands and cities are left astern, your faults will follow you whithersoever you travel."

—*Virgil, from the Roman epic poem "The Aeneid" (19 BC)*

"The wish to travel seems to me characteristically human: the desire to move, to satisfy your curiosity or ease your fears, to change the circumstances of your life...to risk the unknown."

—*Paul Theroux, American author of many books from, "The Tao of Travel" (2011)*

"Travel is the best way we have of rescuing the humanity of places, and saving them from abstraction and ideology."

—*Pico Iyer, American author of many books, from the essay "Why We Travel" on Salon.com (2000)*

"And men go about to wonder at the heights of the mountains, and the mighty waves of the sea, and the wide sweep of rivers, and the circuit of the ocean, and the revolutions of the stars, but themselves they consider not."

—*Augustine of Hippo, aka Saint Augustine, early Christian theologian (354-430), from "The Confessions" (398)*

"For the born traveler, travelling is a besetting vice. Like other vices, it is imperious, demanding its victim's time, money, energy and the sacrifice of comfort."

—*Aldous Huxley (1894-1963), English essayist and author of "Brave New World" (1932)*

"I wasn't a traveler at all, I was just another rubberneck in a city which made its living out of credulous rubbernecks. Go buy a guidebook! Take a buggy ride! Eat *beignets*!"

—*Jonathan Raban, British author and novelist, writing about New Orleans in "Old Glory" (1981)*

"Journeys flower spontaneously out of the demands of our natures—and the best of them lead us not only outwards in space, but inwards as well."

—*Lawrence Durrell (1912-1990), British author and expat best known for his tetralogy "The Alexandria Quartet," from "Bitter Lemons" (1957)*

"I have been a stranger in a strange land."

—*Exodus, 2:22*

"This journey had beggared our language: no words could express its horror...We were beginning to think of death as a friend."

—*Apsley Cherry-Garrard (1886-1959), British member of Robert Falcon Scott's South Pole expedition in 1911-12, from "The Worst Journey in the World" (1922)*

SUMMER

"Know most of the rooms of thy native country before thou goest over the threshold thereof."

—*Thomas Fuller (1608-1661), English preacher, historian and scholar, from "Of Travelling" in "The Holy State and the Profane State" (1642)*

"Why do you wonder that globe-trotting does not help you, seeing that you always take yourself with you? The reason which set you wandering is ever at your heels."

—*Socrates, quoted by Seneca the Younger in "Moral Letters to Lucilius" (64 AD)*

"*To travel hopefully is a better thing than to arrive.*"

—*Robert Louis Stevenson (1850-1894), Scottish novelist best known for the books "Treasure Island," "Kidnapped" and "Strange Case of Dr. Jekyll and Mr. Hyde," from his essay "El Dorado" (1878)*

"Travel is deeply purposeful: as we move through space, we are changed, we discover, and we are transformed."

—*Peter Whitfield, English author, historian and poet, from "Travel, A Literary History" (2011)*

"Travel is glamorous only in retrospect."

—*Paul Theroux, American author of many novels and travel books*

"I have found out that there ain't no surer way to find out whether you like people or hate them than to travel with them."

—*Mark Twain, "Tom Sawyer Abroad" (1894)*

"From the remotest times, it has only been through travel that human understanding improves and culture spreads."

—*Thomas Nugent (ca 1700-1772), Anglo-Irish writer and author of "The Grand Tour" (1749)*

"Unless a person has walked through Rome under the light of a full moon he cannot imagine the beauty of it."

—*Johann Wolfgang von Goethe (1749-1832), German author, poet and politician, from "Italian Journey" (1816)*

"We are all travelers in the wilderness of this world, and the best we can find in our travels is an honest friend."

—*Robert Louis Stevenson (1850-1894), Scottish novelist best known for the books "Treasure Island," "Kidnapped" and "Strange Case of Dr. Jekyll and Mr. Hyde"*

"We live in a wonderful world that is full of beauty, charm and adventure. There is no end to the adventures we can have if only we seek them with our eyes open."

—*Jawaharlal Nehru (1889-1964), first prime minister of India*

"One always begins to forgive a place as soon as it's left behind."

—*Charles Dickens (1812-1870), English author and social critic*

"The only aspect of our travels that is guaranteed to hold an audience is disaster."

—*Martha Gellhorn (1908-1998), American novelist, journalist and third wife of Ernest Hemingway, from "Travels with Myself and Others: A Memoir" (1978)*

"I love to travel, but I hate to arrive."

—*Albert Einstein*

AUTUMN

"The longest journey is the journey inwards."

> —*Dag Hammarskjold (1905-1961), Swedish diplomat, economist, author and the second secretary-general of the United Nations, from Markings (1964)*

"The world may be known without leaving the house."

> —*Lao Tzu (600 BC-531 BC), Chinese Taoist Philosopher, founder of Taoism; Poem 47, "Tao Te Ching" (The Way of Life)*

"We are constantly told that true travel is now dead, killed by the age of mass tourism; but isn't this pure elitism?"

> —*Peter Whitfield, English author, historian and poet, from "Travel, A Literary History" (2011)*

"Delay and dirt are the realities of the most rewarding travel."

—*Paul Theroux, American author of many novels and travel books, from "Ghost Train to the Eastern Star" (2008)*

"Choose your country, use guidebooks to identify the areas most frequented by foreigners—and then go in the opposite direction."

—*Dervla Murphy, Irish author of 23 travel books, including "Full Tilt" (1965)*

"The stars, that nature hung in heaven, and filled their lamps with everlasting oil, to give due light to the misled and lonely traveler."

—*John Milton (1608-1674), from "The Lady Lost in the Wood," "Comus" (1634)*

"Perhaps the only way to experience real wonder and freshness today is to travel without a guidebook."

—*Rory MacLean, British-Canadian author of eleven books, from "Magic Bus" (2006)*

"What gives value to travel is fear... At that moment we are feverish but also porous, so that the slightest touch makes us quiver to the depths of our being."

—*Albert Camus (1913-1960), French Nobel Prize-winning author and philosopher, from "Notebooks 1935-1942"*

"Who can see such trees [redwoods] and bear to be away from them? I must go back. It's not right that I should die under lesser trees."

—*Thomas Merton (1915-1968), American Catholic mystic, Trappist monk, poet and author of "The Seven Storey Mountain (1948)," from "Woods, Shore, Desert: A Notebook, May 1968"*

"Traveling is almost like talking with men of other centuries."

—*René Descartes (1596-1650), French philosopher, mathematician and writer*

"Journeys, like artists, are born and not made. A thousand differing circumstances contribute to them, few of them willed or determined by the will—whatever we may think."

 —*Lawrence Durrell (1912-1990), expatriate British novelist, poet and travel writer best known for his tetralogy of novels, "The Alexandria Quartet" (1957-1960), from "Bitter Lemons" (1957)*

"Two great talkers will not travel far together."

 —*Spanish Proverb*

"The gentle reader will never, never know what a consummate ass he can become, until he goes abroad. I speak now, of course, in the supposition that the gentle reader has not been abroad, and therefore is not already a consummate ass."

 —*Mark Twain, from "The Innocents Abroad" (1869)*

WINTER

"But why oh why do the wrong people travel,
when the right people stay back home?"

—*Noel Coward (1899-1973), English playwright,
composer, director, actor and singer, from his
musical comedy "Sail Away" (1961)*

"We shall not cease from exploration
And the end of all our exploring
Will be to arrive where we started
And know the place for the first time."]

—*T.S. Eliot (1888-1965), American essayist,
publisher, playwright, social critic and poet,
from "Four Quartets" (1942)*

"A good holiday is one that is spent among
people whose notions of time are vaguer
than yours."

—*J.B. Priestley (1894-1984), English novelist,
playwright and broadcaster known for his
morale boosting BBC talks during the Battle
of Britain*

"The question is not what you look at, but what you see."

—*Henry David Thoreau (1817-1862),*
American author of many books including
"Walden," from "Journal," 5 August 1851

"We are all inventors, each sailing out on a voyage of discovery, guided each by a private chart, of which there is no duplicate."

—*Ralph Waldo Emerson (1803-1882),*
American essayist and poet, from "Resources"
(1871)

"A city becomes a world when one loves one of its inhabitants."

—*Lawrence Durrell (1912-1990), expatriate*
British novelist, poet and travel writer best
known for his tetralogy of novels, "The
Alexandria Quartet" (1957-1960), from
"Justine" (1957)

"Travel spoils you for regular life."

—*Bill Barich, American writer, from "Traveling*
Light" (1984)

"There is a third dimension to traveling, the longing for what is beyond."

—*Jan Myrdal, Swedish author and columnist, from "The Silk Road" (1979)*

"In sacred travel, every experience is uncanny. No encounter is without meaning."

—*Phil Cousineau, American author and filmmaker, from "The Art of Pilgrimage" (1998)*

"I see now that my travels as much as the act of writing were ways of escape."

—*Graham Greene (1904-1991), English novelist, from "Ways of Escape" (1980)*

"I have only to go to a different country, sky, language, scenery to feel it is worth living."

—*Martha Gellhorn (1908-1998), American novelist and journalist, from her letters*

"The real meaning of travel, like that of a conversation by the fireside, is the discovery of oneself through contact with other people."

—*Paul Tournier (1898-1986), Swiss physician and author, from "The Meaning of Persons" (1982)*

"When a traveller returneth home, let him not leave the countries where he has travelled altogether behind."

—*Francis Bacon (1561-1626), English philosopher, statesman, scientist, lawyer and pioneer of the scientific method*

SPRING

"No road offers more mystery than the first one you mount from the town you were born to, the first time you mount it of your own volition, on a trip funded by your own coffee tin of wrinkled up dollars."

—*Mary Karr, American poet and essayist best known for her memoir "The Liars' Club," from "Cherry" (2000)*

"Here I am, safely returned over those peaks from a journey far more beautiful and strange than anything I had hoped for or imagined—how is it that this safe return brings such regret?"

—*Peter Mathiesson (1927-2014), American novelist and naturalist and cofounder of "The Paris Review," from "The Snow Leopard" (1978)*

"The rewards of the journey far outweigh the risk of leaving the harbor."

—*Proverb*

"They change their climate, not their soul, who rush across the sea."

—Horace (65 BC-8 BC), Roman lyric poet, from "The Odes of Horace"

"Adventure-travel is any activity used as a conduit to observe, share, enjoy, suffer, encounter, or experience that which is outside the boundaries of one's own day-to-day life."

—Randy Wayne White, American crime novelist and nonfiction adventure writer, from "The Sharks of Lake Nicaragua" (1999)

"True and sincere traveling is no pastime, but it is as serious as the grave."

—Henry David Thoreau (1817-1862), American author of many books including "Walden," from "A Week on the Concord and Merrimack Rivers (1849)

"You'll never meet a traveler who, after five trips, brags, 'I always travel heavier.'"

—Rick Steves, filmmaker, tour guide and author of the best-selling "Rick Steves' Travel Guides," from "Europe through the Back Door" (1998)

"There are map people whose joy is to lavish more attention on the sheets of colored paper than on the colored land rolling by."

—*John Steinbeck (1902-1968), American Nobel Prize winner and author of many books, including "The Grapes of Wrath" (1939), from "Travels with Charley" (1962)*

"We travel for romance, we travel for architecture, and we travel to be lost. There's nothing better than to walk around Paris and not know where in hell you are."

—*Ray Bradbury (1920-2012), American science fiction author of many books, from an interview with Rob Couteau, 1990*

"I think you travel to search and you come back home to find yourself there."

—*Chimimanda Ngozi Adiche, Nigerian novelist, author of "Americanah" (2013), "Half of a Yellow Sun" (2006) and "Purple Hibiscus" (2003)*

"I may not have gone where I intended to go, but I think I have ended up where I intended to be."

—*Douglas Adams (1952-2001), English writer, humorist and dramatist best known for a BBC radio comedy and series of five books titled "The Hitchhiker's Guide to the Galaxy" (1978-1992)*

"Good company in a journey makes the way to seem shorter."

—*Italian proverb quoted by English writer Izaak Walton (1594-1683) in "The Compleat Angler" (1653)*

"I should like well enough to spend the whole of my in life traveling abroad, if I could anywhere borrow another life to spend afterwards at home!"

—*William Hazlitt (1778-1830), English literary critic and philosopher, from "On Going a Journey" in "Table Talk" (1822)*

SUMMER

"I can't think of anything that excites a greater sense of childlike wonder than to be in a country where you are ignorant of almost everything."

—*Bill Bryson, American expat writer living in England, author of many books, from "Neither Here Nor There: Travels in Europe" (1992)*

"Rich and happy as I was after my third voyage, I could not make up my mind to stay at home altogether."

—*"The Arabian Nights: Tales from One Thousand and One Nights" (c. 1000), "The Seven Voyages of Sinbad the Sailor"*

"A person needs at intervals to separate from family and companions and go to new places. One must go without familiars in order to be open to influences, to change."

—*Katharine Butler Hathaway (1890-1942), American author, from "The Little Locksmith" (1943)*

"Venture all; see what fate brings."

—*Vietnamese Proverb*

"Traveling always entails infidelity. You do your best to mask the feeling of sly triumph that comes with turning your back on home and all it stands for."

—*Jonathan Raban, British author and novelist, from "Passage to Juneau" (1999)*

"Travel was an antidote to an overdose of stability."

—*Bill Barich, American writer, from "Traveling Light" (1984)*

"Most people have that fantasy of catching the train that whistles in the night."

—*Willie Nelson, American musician-singer-songwriter, from "Willie: An Autobiography" (1988)*

"Traveling makes men wiser, but less happy."

—*Thomas Jefferson, from a letter in 1787*

"Through travel I first became aware of the outside world; it was through travel that I found my own introspective way into becoming a part of it."

—*Eudora Welty (1909-2001), Pulitzer Prize-winning American author of novels and short stories, from "One Writer's Beginnings" (1984)*

"He said he wanted to slow life up and quite rightly felt that by traveling he would make time move with less rapidity."

—*Graham Greene (1904-1991), English novelist, from "Travels with My Aunt" (1969)*

"Some people look for a beautiful place. Others make a place beautiful."

—*Hazrat Inayat Khan (1882-1927), Indian classical musician and founder of The Sufi Order in the West (1914)*

"If the essence of travel is the inner journey, then the experience of foreign places can still be a transforming one."

   —*Peter Whitfield, English author, historian and poet, from "Travel, A Literary History" (2011)*

"Even disasters—there are always disasters when you travel—can be turned into adventures."

   —*Marilyn French (1929-2009), American author best known for her novel "The Women's Room" (1977), and "From Eve to Dawn: A History of Women" (2003)*

AUTUMN

"There are pioneer souls that blaze their paths where highways never ran."

—Sam Walter Foss (1858-1911), from "The House by the Side of the Road" (1899)

"A border is always a temptation."

—Larry McMurtry, American novelist and screenwriter, from "In a Narrow Grave: Essays on Texas" (1983)

"Going up that river was like travelling back to the earliest beginnings of the world, when vegetation rioted on the earth and the big trees were kings."

—Joseph Conrad (1857-1924), Russian-born Polish novelist who wrote in English, from "Heart of Darkness" (1899)

"The stride of passengers off an airplane is always jauntier than the stride on."

—Tom Clancy (1947-2013), American novelist, from "Patriot Games" (1987)

"Most travelers content themselves with what they may chance to see from car-windows, hotel verandas, or the deck of a steamer...clinging to the battered highways like drowning sailors to a life-raft."

—*John Muir, (1838-1914), American naturalist, from "The Basin of the Columbia River" (1888)*

"I had once spread my wings, and now that I had returned to my nest again, I was dissatisfied."

—*Richard Halliburton (1900-1939), American writer and adventurer, from "The Glorious Adventure" (1927)*

"My favorite thing is to go where I have never gone."

—*Diane Arbus (1923-1971), American photographer and writer best known for her photographs of marginalized people, from "Diane Arbus: Monograph" (1972)*

"He who would travel happily must travel light."

—*Antoine de Saint-Exupery (1900-1944), French writer, poet and aviator best known for his fable "The Little Prince" (1943)*

"I was drunk with travel, dizzy with the import of it all, and indifferent to thoughts of home and family."

—*Charles Kuralt (1934-1997), American journalist best known for his "On the Road" series for CBS Evening News with Walter Cronkite, from "A Life on the Road" (1990)*

"A good traveler does not much mind the uninteresting places."

—*Freya Stark (1893-1993), British adventurer and author of more than two dozen travel books, from "Alexander's Path" (1958)*

"I have traveled, in one way or another, all my life. I have loved every moment of it, and fully intend to go on until I drop."

—*John Julius Norwich, English historian, writer and TV personality, from "A Taste for Travel" (1985)*

"A traveler who leaves the journey open to the road finds unforeseen things come to shape it."

—*William Least Heat-Moon, American writer, from "Blue Highways" (1982)*

"It's the one thing you say about going to the end of the road: when you start making your way back to civilization, you don't need the rearview mirror. Ain't nothing gaining on you."

—*Tim Cahill, American essayist and author of many books, including "Lost in My Own Backyard" (2004), from "Road Fever" (1991)*

WINTER

"I have changed my habits with the hemispheres, but there is still some internal rhythm that comes alive in April."

—*Tony Horwitz, American Pulitzer Prize-winning journalist and author of several books, from "One for the Road" (1987)*

"Once you have traveled, the voyage never ends, but is played out over and over again in the quietest chambers."

—*Pat Conroy (1945-2016), American author of the novel "The Great Santini" (1976) and the memoir "My Losing Season" (2002), from "The Prince of Tides" (1986)*

"A trip, a safari, an exploration, is an entity, different from all other journeys. It has personality, temperament, individuality, uniqueness."

—*John Steinbeck (1902-1968), American Nobel Prize winner and author of many books, including "The Grapes of Wrath" (1939), from "Travels with Charley" (1962)*

"Your travel life has the essence of a dream. It is something outside the normal, yet you are in it. It is peopled with characters you have never seen before and in all probability will never see again."

—*Agatha Christie (1890-1976), English author and creator of the Hercule Poirot and Jane Marple mysteries*

"A good holiday is one spent among people whose notions of time are vaguer than yours."

—*J.B. Priestly (1894-1984), English novelist, playwright, social commentator and broadcaster known for his novel "The Good Companions" (1929) and his morale-boosting BBC broadcasts during WWII*

ACKNOWLEDGMENTS

I'd like to thank Spud Hilton, travel editor of the *San Francisco Chronicle*, for his patience and support over the five and a half years he ran "The Quotable Traveler" in his Sunday Travel section. I was and am always proud to be included in those pages. Thanks also to Bonnie Smetts, friend and colleague, for pulling the documents into shape and giving these words a grander resonance through her elegant design. Many thanks also to the countless web resources, libraries, and bookstores that aided me in my quest. And most special thanks to the wide universe of writers and travelers whose inspiring words fill these pages. They have made the world a much more special place with their presence.

ABOUT THE EDITOR

Larry Habegger is a writer and editor who has been covering the world since his international travels began in the 1970s. As a freelance writer for more than three decades, his work has appeared in many major newspapers and magazines, including the *Los Angeles Times*, *Chicago Tribune*, *Travel & Leisure*, and *Outside*. His newspaper column "World Travel Watch" was syndicated for 31 years and during that time ran in major papers in five countries. In 1993 he cofounded the award-winning Travelers' Tales Books with James and Tim O'Reilly, where he serves as executive editor and helps oversee the company's publishing program and has worked on all of its 130-plus books. Larry teaches the craft of memoir and the personal essay and runs several writers groups. He is also a founder of The Prose Doctors, an editors consortium; editor of the annual magazine *The Travel Guide to California*; and editor in chief of Triporati. com, a destination discovery site.

CPSIA information can be obtained
at www.ICGtesting.com
Printed in the USA
BVOW06s2252301216
472322BV00001B/1/P